The Czech Christmas Cookbook

Lucie Rogers

Contents

Introduction

Christmas is very popular in the Czech Republic. The wintery climate of the country and central European setting gives a very traditional festive atmosphere to the Christmas period.

The Czechs have many of the usual Christmas traditions such as special meals over Christmas - the Czech's main day is 24th December - Christmas markets, parties, family gatherings, decorations, carols and gift giving. There are also a number of unique and rather strange Czech traditions and superstitions over the period.

Naturally food plays a big part of the Czech Christmas with people overindulging in a wide range of foods. Traditional Czech foods such as fried carp, schnitzel, dumplings, soups, smoked and roast meats and cabbage dishes are eaten. Czech Christmas cookies are famous.

Try some Czech Christmas food with this book.

Fried Cheese

Ingredients

slices of Edam cheese
flour
beaten egg
breadcrumbs
oil

Put the cheese in flour, then egg, then breadcrumbs.

Fry in oil on all sides until browned.

Serve with boiled potatoes and tartare sauce.

Sauerkraut Soup

Ingredients

400g/14 oz of sauerkraut
half a chopped onion
4 chopped potatoes
1 teaspoon of caraway seed
2 tablespoons of sour cream
salt
pepper
oil
sausage pieces e.g. kielbasa (optional)

Cook the onions in some oil on a low heat for 8 minutes. Add the potatoes, 240ml/1 cup of water, caraway seed and some salt. Cook for 5 minutes.

Add the sauerkraut.

Cook for 20 minutes - until potatoes are cooked. Add the sausage half way through cooking if using. Add sour cream.

Cauliflower Pancakes

Ingredients

1 cauliflower cut into florets
2 egg whites
2 egg yolks
salt
pepper
4 tablespoons of flour
vegetable oil

Put the cauliflower in a pan of salted boiling water. Cook on a low heat for 7 minutes.

Drain the cauliflower then mash it. Add the yolk and mix. Add the flour and some salt and pepper and mix.

Whisk the egg whites, then fold them into the cauliflower.

Put spoonfuls of the mix in hot oil and fry until golden brown on both sides.

Pickled Cheese

Ingredients

slices of Camembert cheese or Czech equivalent
3 chopped onions
7 minced of garlic
allspice berries
peppercorns
chilli peppers
salt
vegetable oil
paprika

Coat the cheese in garlic, salt and paprika.

Take a glass jar (e.g. a mason jar) and put some onion, peppercorns and allspice berries in the bottom. Add 3 slices of cheese and some chilli peppers. Repeat layers to fill the jar.

Pour in some oil. put a lid on the jar and place in the refrigerator for 3 days.

Serve with bread.

Dill Spread

Ingredients

2 tablespoons of chopped fresh dill
half a finely chopped onion
100g/3.5 oz of cream cheese
130g/4.6 oz of cottage cheese
1 tablespoon of lemon juice
100g/3.5 oz of butter
salt
pepper

Mix the cheeses, lemon juice, butter and some salt and pepper in a bowl. Add the dill and onion and mix.

Fish Soup

Ingredients

283g/10 oz of fish pieces
3 fish heads
1 chopped onion
1 chopped carrot
2 chopped sticks of celery
2 chopped cloves of garlic
2 tablespoons of flour
8 peppercorns
4 allspice berries
240ml/1 cup of milk
3 tablespoons of butter
salt
1 tablespoon of chopped chives
butter

Place the fish heads in a pan containing 5 cups of boiling salted water. Add half the onion. Boil, then cook on a low heat for 35 minutes. Strain the soup keeping the liquid.

Cook the rest of the onion in some butter in a saucepan for 8 minutes. Add the flour and garlic and simmer for 6 minutes stirring all the time. Add the other liquid, fish pieces, carrot, celery, allspice and peppercorns. Add the milk, and cook on a low heat for 10 minutes.

Add some salt and pepper and garnish with chives.

Mushroom Soup

Ingredients

255g/9 oz of chopped mushrooms
5 chopped potatoes
2 tablespoons of chopped fresh dill
1 teaspoon of caraway seeds
2 allspice berries
2 teaspoons of sugar
3 tablespoons of flour
1 litre/4 cups of hot vegetable stock/broth
7 tablespoons of butter
240ml/1 cup of sour cream
salt
pepper
white vinegar (optional)
hard boiled egg slices
vegetable oil

Cook the mushrooms in some vegetable oil for 6 minutes.

Put the butter in a saucepan with the rest of the sunflower oil. Add the flour and mix, then cook for 5 minutes stirring all the time. Add the vegetable stock and whisk. Add the mushrooms, potatoes, allspice and caraway. Cover the pan then cook on a medium heat for 15 minutes - until potatoes are cooked.

Remove the allspice from the pan. Add the sour cream and cook for 2 minutes stirring all the time.

Add some salt and pepper, the dill and the sugar. 2 tablespoons of white vinegar can be added if wanted.

Garnish the soup with sliced hard boiled egg.

Flatbread

Ingredients

130ml/half a cup of buttermilk
240g/8.4 oz of flour
80g/2.8 oz of lard
half a teaspoon of salt
1 teaspoon of baking soda
caraway seeds
sea salt
oil or lard

Put buttermilk. flour, lard, salt and baking soda in a bowl and mix. Make a dough.

Make flat circles from the dough. Spread a little oil or lard on top. Sprinkle with caraway seeds and some sea salt.

Put on a baking tray and cook in a preheated oven at 400F for 20 minutes.

Czech Christmas Trivia

Traditionally, Czech Christmas dinner on 24 December is served after sunset - not until the first star has come out.

A traditional Czech Christmas dinner is mushroom, fish or sauerkraut soup followed by fried carp with potato salad.

Those who do not like carp eat another fish such as salmon or a dish such as pork or chicken schnitzel.

Czech Christmas cookies - Vánoční cukroví - are a big part of Christmas. There are many recipes, and each family have their own special family recipes.

Potato salad is normally eaten for Christmas dinner on 24 December. Each family has their own recipe.

Apple Strudel is a popular dessert for the Czech Christmas dinner on December 24. It is served with whipped cream.

Potatoes with Zucchini

Ingredients

4 cubed potatoes
2 cubed zucchini/courgette
1 chopped onion
1 egg yolk
260ml/1 cup of milk
3 tablespoons of sour cream
1 teaspoon of caraway seeds
half a teaspoon of paprika
1 bay leaf
butter
flour
pepper
2 tablespoons of chopped dill
boiled egg

Put the zucchini and potato in a pan. Cover with water. Add some salt and the paprika and bring to the boil, then cook on a low heat for 8 minutes. Drain.

Put the onion in a pan with some butter and cook for 4 minutes. Add a tablespoon of flour and mix, then add the milk. Stir to make sauce then add the zucchini and potato.

Mix the sour cream, yolk and dill. Add to the vegetables and cook on a low heat for 6 minutes.

Garnish with boiled egg.

Red Cabbage

Ingredients

450g/1 lb of sliced red cabbage
1 chopped onion
1 teaspoon of caraway seeds
1 tablespoon of flour
100g/half a cup of sugar
half a teaspoon of pepper
1 teaspoon of salt
130ml/4.3 fl oz of apple cider vinegar
butter

Cook the onion in some butter for 6 minutes.

Add the vinegar, sugar, salt, pepper and 240ml/1 cup of water. Bring to the boil. Add the cabbage and caraway seeds. Bring to the boil then cook on a low heat for 30 minutes.

Add the flour, stir and cook for 2 more minutes.

Stuffed Pepper

Ingredients

720g/1.6 lb of ground/minced beef
6 bell peppers
2 chopped onions
200g/1 cup of cooked rice
1 egg
1kg/40 oz of chopped tomatoes
2 teaspoons of dried oregano
140ml/1 cup of sour cream
2 peppercorns
1 tablespoon of fresh parsley
salt
pepper
oil

Cook half the onion in a pan in some oil for 7 minutes.

Mix the cooked onion, beef, rice and eggs in a bowl. Add the parsley and some salt and pepper. Stuff the peppers with the mix. Put the peppers in a baking dish.

Put the rest of the onion in a pan and cook in some oil for 7 minutes. Add the tomatoes, oregano and peppercorns. Cook on a low heat for 20 minutes. Pour the mix over the peppers.

Bake in a preheated oven at 176C/350F for 1 and a half hours.

Take the peppers out the dish. Take rest of the contents of the pan and blend or rub through a sieve. Put the sauce in a pan and cook for 7 minutes. Stir in the sour cream and serve over the peppers.

Cucumbers with Sour Cream

Ingredients

2 peeled and sliced cucumbers
1 chopped clove of garlic
1 sliced onion
4 tablespoons of sour cream
1 tablespoon of white vinegar
half a teaspoon of paprika
half a teaspoon of salt

Mix the cucumber, garlic and salt. Leave for 30 minutes,

Squeeze the cucumber gently to remove excess moisture. Mix the cucumber with the onion, vinegar and sour cream. Sprinkle the paprika over the top.

Vegetable Soup

Zeleninová polévka

Ingredients

half a chopped onion
2 chopped carrots
2 chopped potatoes
1 chopped stick of celery
1 chopped kohlrabi
4 peppercorns
2 chopped cloves of garlic
salt
2 tablespoons of buckwheat

Put the carrot and onion in a saucepan with some butter. Cook for 4 minutes.

Add the potato, celery and kohlrabi. Pour in 1.5 litres/6 cups of hot water. Add the peppercorn, buckwheat and some salt. Cover and cook on a medium heat for 25 minutes.

Add the garlic. Garnish with chopped spinach leaves.

Potato Sauce

Ingredients

4 peeled and chopped potatoes
1 finely chopped onion
3 beaten eggs
230ml/1 cup of milk
120g/4 oz of flour
1 tablespoon of butter
half a teaspoon of caraway seeds
half a teaspoon of crushed black pepper
800ml/1 and one third of a cup of vegetable stock/broth
1 teaspoon of salt

Put the stock in a pan. Add the caraway seeds, salt, pepper, butter, onions and potatoes. Bring to the boil.

Mix the milk with 200ml/7 fl oz of hot water. Add the flour and mix well. Add this mix to the pan and whisk to make a sauce.

Cook the mix on a low heat for 25 minutes - until potatoes are cooked.

Take off the heat. Add the eggs and whisk. Add some salt and pepper.

Serve with bread or dumplings.

Open Faced Sandwich

Obložené Chlebíčky

Ingredients

baguette slices
anchovy butter
horseradish cream
salami slices
ham slices
smoked turkey slices
olives
pickled beetroot slices
sliced scallions/spring onions
pickles
cheese - such as Cheddar or Gruyère
anchovies
sardines
smoked salmon
hard boiled egg slices
chopped fresh herbs - such as chives or dill

Spread some anchovy paste or horseradish cream on the bread slices.

Top with other ingredients of your choice.

Horseradish Cream

Ingredients

1 and a half tablespoons of grated horseradish
1 tablespoon of white wine vinegar
160ml/5.4 fl oz of double cream
half a teaspoon of mustard powder
half a teaspoon of caster sugar
salt
pepper

Put the horseradish in some hot water for 15 minutes Drain.

Mix the horseradish with the other ingredients. Place in the refrigerator for 1 hour.

Open Faced Sandwich

Chicken Schnitzel

Anchovy Butter

Ingredients

anchovy paste
butter

Mix some butter with some anchovy paste in a bowl.

Mayonnaise Salad

Ingredients

160g/5.6 oz of sliced ham
80g/2.8 oz of peas
200g/7 oz of plain mayonnaise
1 finely chopped onion
100g/3.5 oz of sliced pickles
pepper
salt

Put the ingredients in a pan and mix well.

Serve with white bread.

Tartare Sauce

Ingredients

2 finely chopped pickles
half a finely chopped onion
half a teaspoon of sugar
260ml/9 fl oz of mayonnaise
1 teaspoon of Dijon mustard
salt
pepper

Mix the pickles, onion, sugar, mayonnaise and mustard in a bowl. Add some salt and pepper.

Czech Christmas Trivia

Put the pickles, onion, sugar, mayonnaise, mustard and some salt in a bowl. Mix well. Place in the refrigerator for 1 hour. Add some pepper.

Vánočka, a sweet Christmas bread is eaten during the Christmas season as part of Christmas dinner on 24 December and as part of various festive breakfasts. It is served dry or with butter or jam. Another popular dish made with the bread is French toast for breakfast.

On 24 December during Christmas dinner Little Jesus (Ježíšek) puts presents under the Christmas tree rather than Santa Clause/Father Christmas. Presents are opened after dinner. No one is sure what the mysterious Ježíšek looks like.

There is a tradition that whoever sees a vision of a golden piglet on Christmas eve will have a prosperous New Year. In order to see the piglet, meat is not allowed to be consumed during the daytime on December 24.

Eggnog is a very popular drink in the Czech Republic at Christmas time. As well as being drunk on its own, it is also used in other food and drink items such as being added to coffee or ice cream.

Potato Pancakes

Ingredients

800g/1.7 lb of grated potato
2 eggs
1 chopped onion
68g/half a cup flour
60g/half a cup of farina
half a teaspoon of caraway seeds
60ml/a quarter cup of milk
salt
pepper
oil

Cook the onion in some oil on a low heat for 30 minutes,

Mix the eggs, milk, flour, farina, caraway seeds, onion and some salt and pepper in a bowl.

Heat up some oil in a pan. Put spoonfuls of the mix in the oil and cook for 5 minutes on each side.

Potato Salad with Root Vegetables

Bramborový salát

Ingredients

700g/1 and a half lb of potato (a "salad" variety such as new potato or a "waxy" variety)
3 chopped hard boiled eggs
half a chopped celeriac
half a chopped onion
70g/half a cup of peas
1 chopped cucumber
1 chopped pickle
60g/2.1 oz of chopped parsley
115g/half a cup of mayonnaise
1 tablespoon of mustard
chopped ham or salami (optional)
salt
pepper

Put the celeriac in a pan of hot water and cook for five minutes. Drain.

Put then potatoes in a pn of hot water and cook for 12 minutes. Drain and chop.

Mix the ingredients gently in a bowl.

Caper Sauce

Ingredients

55g/2 oz bacon
1 chopped onion
2 tablespoons of capers
2 tablespoons of Dijon mustard
118ml/4 fl oz of sour cream
1 tablespoon of flour
salt
pepper
butter

Cook the bacon and onion in some butter in a pan for 6
minutes. Add the mustard, capers and 2 tablespoons of water.
Cook on a low heat for 5 minutes.

Mix the cream with the flour. Add to the pan, boil, then cook
on a low heat stirring all the time until the sauce has thickened

Dumpling

Carp with Potato Salad

Dumpling

Knedliky

Ingredients

380g/13 oz of flour
400g/14 oz of dried bread cubes
3 beaten eggs
1 teaspoon of baking soda/sodium carbonate
1 teaspoon of baking powder
half a teaspoon of salt
half a teaspoon of sugar
1 cup/240ml of milk

Mix the flour, baking powder, baking soda, sugar and salt in a bowl. Add the eggs and milk. Mix and make a dough.

Knead the dough for 5 minutes. Fold in the dried bread. shape into bread loaf shapes

Put the dough in a pan of boiling water. Cook on a low heat for 30 minutes. Place the dumpling on a plate. cut into slices to serve.

Mushroom and Barley Kuba

Ingredients

70g/2.4 oz of dried mushrooms
210g/7.4 oz of pearl barley
2 chopped onions
2 chopped cloves of garlic
1 teaspoon of cumin
260ml/1 cup of vegetable stock
butter
salt
pepper

Put the mushrooms in 420ml/1 and three quarters of a cup of water. Leave for 8 hours.

Put the pearl barley in a bowl and cover with water. Leave for 8 hours.

Drain the mushrooms - keep the water.

Drain the barley.

Put the barley in a pan with some butter and cook for 5 minutes. Add the mushroom water and cook for 5 minutes. Add the stock, then cook on a low heat for 45 minutes - until the barley is cooked.

Chop the mushrooms and cook on a medium heat in some butter with the onion, garlic, cumin and some salt and pepper for 6 minutes. Mix this mix with the barley.

Grease a baking dish with some butter. Add the barley mix and cook in a preheated oven at 180C/356F for 30 minutes.

Cauliflower and Egg

Ingredients

1 cauliflower
4 beaten eggs
1 chopped onion
2 teaspoons of caraway seeds
butter
salt
pepper

Take the green leaves off the cauliflower. Place in a pan of boiling salted water. Cover and cook on a low heat for 6 minutes - until cooked.

Drain and break into florets.

Put the onion in a pan with some butter and fry for 5 minutes. Add the caraway seeds and cauliflower and cook for 5 minutes. Add the egg with some salt and pepper and stir. Cook on a low heat, stirring constantly, for 7 minutes - until eggs are cooked.

Mushrooms with Caraway

Ingredients

500g/1.1 lb of sliced mushrooms
half a chopped medium sized onion
1 teaspoon of caraway seeds
butter
salt

Cook the onions in some butter for 6 minutes. Add the
mushrooms and caraway seeds and bring the mix to the boil.
Cook for 6 minutes on a medium heat. Add some salt.

Green Beans with Paprika

Ingredients

450g/1 lb of chopped green beans
half a chopped onion
1 tablespoon of paprika
2 tablespoons of flour
1 teaspoon of salt
butter
240ml/1 cup of sour cream

Fill a pan with water and bring to the boil. Add the salt and the beans. Boil, then cook on a medium heat for 15 minutes. Drain.

Cook the onions in some butter for 6 minutes. Take off the heat and add the paprika and mix.

Mix the sour cream and onion. Add to the pan with the onions. Cook on a low heat for 6 minutes. Stir, then add the beans. Cook on low heat for 6 minutes.

Czech Christmas Food Trivia

During Christmas a fried wine sausage is served with mashed potatoes.

A Czech Christmas tradition is to slice an apple in half, and if the core is star shaped that mean happiness; a cross shaped core means something bad will happen.

Pets are fed after Christmas dinner on 24 December. If they are not it is considered bad luck!

A Czech Christmas dinner tradition is to place coins under the plates at the table. Whoever has the most money will earn the most money in the following year.

The table at Christmas dinner is set for an even number of people, even if there are an off number of diners. This is because an odd number of plates is considered unlucky.

Cabbage with Caraway

Ingredients

1 chopped cabbage
1 chopped onion
1 tablespoon of caraway seeds
4 tablespoons of sugar
200ml/6.5 fl oz of vinegar
1 tablespoon of flour
salt
oil

Put the cabbage caraway seeds and 2 and a half tablespoons of salt in a pan of water Bring to the boil, then cook on a medium heat for 6 minutes - until cooked.

Celeriac Schnitzel

Ingredients

1 celeriac/celery root cut into thin slices
dried breadcrumbs
1 egg
240ml/1 cup of milk
70g/half a cup of flour
salt
pepper

Mix the milk, egg, flour and some salt and pepper in a bowl.
Coat the celeriac in the flour mix, then coat in breadcrumbs.

Dip the celeriac slices in the flour, then the egg, then the
breadcrumbs.

Fry the slices in hot oil on both sides until golden brown.

Fried Carp

Ingredients

4 carp fillets
flour
eggs
dried breadcrumbs
oil
salt
2 egg
3 tablespoons of milk

Mix the eggs with the milk. Put the flour on a plate. Put the breadcrumbs on another plate.

Add some salt to the carp. Put in the flour, then the egg and then the breadcrumbs.

Fry in hot oil on both sides until browned - about 8 minutes on each side.

Roast Goose

Ingredients

1 goose
1.3kg/3 lb of sauerkraut
2 cored and chopped apples
155g/1 cup of grated potato
1 chopped onion
1 tablespoon of caraway seeds
salt
pepper
butter

Put the sauerkraut and onions in a pan with some butter and cook for 10 minutes. Put in a bowl with the potato, apple, caraway seeds and some pepper. Stuff the goose with the mix.

Put the goose on a rack in a roasting pan. Cook in a preheated oven at 162C/325F for 2 and a half hours, removing the duck fat several times.

Leave to rest for 20 minutes before carving.

Mushroom and Barley Kuba

Christmas Bread

Roast Turkey with Caraway

Ingredients

1 turkey
2 tablespoons of caraway seed
salt
pepper
stock/bouillon cubes
fresh dill

Put the turkey in a roasting dish. Coat the turkey in the
caraway seeds and some salt and pepper. Put two
stock/bouillon cubes in the dish.

Place in a preheated oven at 190C/375F and cook for about 2
and a half hours (15 minutes per gram/lb of turkey).

Strain the juices from the pan into a saucepan. Add a
tablespoon of flour, half a tablespoon of chopped fresh dill and
cook on a medium heat for 7 minutes stirring all the time until
thickened. Serve with the turkey.

Wine Sausage

Ingredients

540g/1.2 kg of chopped beef
540g/1.2 kg of chopped pork
7 slices of toasted bread
1 teaspoon of mace
2 tablespoons of lemon juice
250ml/1 cup of milk
200ml/6.7 fl oz of wine (dry white)
600ml/2 and a half cups of ice water
2 and a half tablespoons of salt
half a teaspoon of white pepper

Season the meat with the salt. Put in the refrigerator for 6 hours.

Put the bread in a bowl with the wine.

Mix the meat, bread and wine mix, milk, pepper, mace and lemon in a bowl. Put the mix through a meat grinder. Put the mix in a bowl and stir in the cold water.

Stuff into sausage casings, or shape into sausage shapes. If not using casings, wrap in clingfilm/plastic wrap. Put in a pan of warm water and cook for 15 minutes.

Take the clingfilm off the sausages and fry them in a pan of oil until golden brown and cooked

Czech Christmas Food Trivia

No one has their back to the door during Christmas dinner - it is considered unlucky.

There is a tradition to bury any leftovers from Christmas dinner in an orchard to help the trees bear fruit the following year.

One strange Czech Christmas tradition is to throw a shoe out the door. If the toe of the shoe is pointing towards the doorway your will get married in the new year!

A Czech Christmas tradition is to put honey on the face which is said to make the person who has honey on their face popular.

Many Czechs have carp for Christmas dinner. Some buy a live carp from the market – there is a tradition where some buy a live carp and keep it in the bath until needed for Christmas. Many choose to just buy a frozen carp.

Pork Burgers

Ingredients

400g/14 oz of minced/ground pork
1 teaspoon of paprika
1 teaspoon of salt
2 slices of white bread
oil

Put the bread in some water and leave for 15 minutes. Squeeze out the water.

Mix the pork, salt, paprika and 50ml of cold water. Add the bread and mix well.

Make into burger shapes and cook in a little oil for 4 minutes on each side - until cooked.

Serve in rye bread or with mashed potatoes.

Steak with Capers

Ingredients

450g/1 lb of steak
85g/3 oz of bacon
1 chopped onion
2 tablespoons of capers
2 tablespoons of butter
2 tablespoons of Dijon mustard
118ml/quarter of a pint sour cream
1 tablespoon of flour
salt
pepper

Add some flour, salt and pepper to the steaks.

Cut the steak into four pieces.

Cook the bacon and onion in the butter fir 4 minutes. Add the steak and cook on both sides for 4 minutes.

Add the mustard, capers and 200ml/7 fl oz of water. Cover the pan and cook on a low heat for 10 minutes - until steaks are cooked.

Put the steak on a plate. Add the cream and flour to the sauce, bring to the boil, then cook on a low heat for 10 minutes- until the sauce thickens.

Serve the steak with the sauce.

Pork in Cream Sauce

Ingredients

1 kg/2.2 lb of pork
160g/5.6 oz of chopped bacon
130g4.5 oz of chopped celeriac/celery root
270g/9.5 oz of chopped carrots
270g/9.5 oz of chopped onion
6 peppercorns
4 allspice berries
2 bay leaves
130g/4.5 oz of parsley
1 teaspoon of chopped fresh thyme
180ml/3 quarters of a cup of cream
1 sliced lemon - with peel removed
2 teaspoons of mustard
5 tablespoons of sugar
salt
oil

Put the pork and bacon in a pan with some oil and cook for 7 minutes. take the pork out of the pan.

Add the onion, carrot and celery root to the pan with the bacon and cook for 7 minutes. Add the bay leaves, peppercorns and allspice berries. add the sugar and cook for 5 minutes. Add the mustard and lemon slices.

Add 2 cups of water and put the pork in the pan. Bring to the boil, then cover and cook on a low heat for 1 hour 40 minutes - until pork is cooked.

Take the pork out and put on a plate. Slice the pork. Remove the allspice berries, peppercorns and bay leaves. Put the sauce in a blender and mix to make a smooth sauce. Stir in the sour cream. Serve sauce over the pork. Garish with cranberry sauce, whipped cream and lemon slices.

Chicken Schnitzel

Ingredients

4 chicken breasts (with bones taken out)
beaten eggs
flour
dried breadcrumbs
salt
oil

Put the chicken between two pieces of plastic wrap/clingfilm.
Beat them with a meat hammer or rolling pin until they are
flat.

Put the eggs in a bow and add a little salt. Put the breadcrumbs
and flour on separate plates.

Dip the chicken in the flour, then egg, then the breadcrumbs.

Heat some oil in a pan, then fry the chicken for 4 minutes on
each side on a medium heat.

Roast Pork

Ingredients

4 lb/1.8kg pork roast
2 chopped onions
2 tablespoons of caraway seeds
1 tablespoon of mustard
270ml/9 fl oz of beer
salt
pepper
3 tablespoons of oil

Mix the oil, mustard and caraway seeds with some salt and pepper. Rub over the pork. Leave for 40 minutes.

Put the onions in a roasting pan and pour over the beer. Put the pork on top. Cover with tin foil then cook in a preheated oven at 176C/350F for 1 hour. Remove the foil. Turn over the pork and cook for 2 hours 40 minutes.

Linzer Cookies

Ingredients

266g/9 oz of flour
160g/5.6 oz of almonds
250g/8.8 oz of butter
4 tablespoons of confectioners'/icing sugar
2 egg yolks
1 tablespoon of lemon zest
2 drops of vanilla essence
raspberry or redcurrant jam

Put the almonds on a sheet and bake in a medium oven for 10 minutes.

Mix the flour with the lemon zest and a pinch of salt.

Put the almonds in a blender with half of sugar and blend.

Mix the rest of the sugar with the butter in a bowl to make a paste. Add the egg yolks and vanilla essence and mix well. Add the flour and almond mix and make a dough.

Cover the dough in clingfilm/plastic wrap and place in the refrigerator for 8 hours.

Roll out the dough. Cut into cookie shapes. Make sure there is a bottom half with no hole and a top half with a hole for each cookie. Roll out unused dough to make more cookies.

Put the cookies on a baking sheet and cook in a preheated oven at 176C/350F for 10 minutes.

Leave to cool. Spread jam on the bottom intact half of each cookie. Put the other halves - with the hole - on the top of the cookies. Dust with powdered sugar.

Beehive Cookies

Ingredients

dough

400g/3 and half cups of vanilla wafer cookies such as Nilla wafers or ladyfingers.
260g/2 cups of confectioners'/icing sugar
2 tablespoons of water
115g/half a cup of butter
60ml/a quarter of a cup of rum
3 tablespoons of cocoa powder

filling

115g/half a cup of butter
65g/half a cup of confectioners'/icing sugar
1 tablespoon of rum
1 tablespoon of condensed milk
1 egg yolk
wafer cookies crumbs
cocoa powder
confectioners'/icing sugar

Mix the dough ingredients in a bowl to make a dough. Place in the refrigerator for 1 hour.

For the filling, mix the butter with the sugar. Add the milk, wafer cookie crumbs, rum and egg yolk and mix.

Take a mould - in a beehive shape for example - and grease with some butter. Add some cocoa and confectioners' sugar. Put some dough in the mould and close the mould. Put a hole in the dough and pipe in some of the filling. Remove the mould. Repeat the process to make the cookies.

Kolaches

Beehive Cookies

Kolaches

Ingredients

160ml/5.5 fl oz of milk
270g/2 cups of flour
6 tablespoons of butter
2 egg yolks
2 teaspoons of dry yeast
2 tablespoons of sugar
half a teaspoon of salt

filling

113g/4 oz cream cheese
3 tablespoons of powdered sugar
apricot jam
6 destoned prunes
1 tablespoon of honey

Put the prunes in a saucepan with the honey. Add 100ml of water and cook high heat for 10 minutes. Mix the cream cheese and powdered sugar to make a paste.

Put the milk in a pan cook for 7 minutes to warm. Add the yeast, sugar and half the flour. Mix, then leave in a warm place until doubled in size.

Mix the butter and egg yolks. Add the dough, salt and rest of the flour, Mix to make a dough. Knead for 12 minutes. Put the dough in a greased bowl, cover with clingfilm or a damp tea towel and leave to double in size in a warm place.

Cut the dough into 12 pieces. Roll the pieces to make circle shapes. Place on a baking sheet and leave in a warm place to double in size.

Make a hole in the top of the dough pieces. Stuff 4 with the prune mix, 4 with the cream cheese mix and 4 with the apricot jam. Place on a baking sheet and cook in a preheated oven at 190C/375F for 20 minutes - until browned.

Apple Strudel

Ingredients

700g/1 and half lb of chopped peeled and cored apple - green
apple such as granny smith or Bramley
80g/2.8 oz of sugar
70g/2.4 oz of raisins
butter
40g/1.4 oz of breadcrumbs
1 teaspoon of cinnamon
1 tablespoon of lemon zest
1 tablespoon of lemon juice
6 filo pastry sheets
icing sugar

Mix the apples, lemon zest, cinnamon, raisins and sugar in a
bowl.

Put a little butter in a pan and cook the breadcrumbs on a
medium heat for 6 minutes. Add the breadcrumbs to the
apples.

Put a sheet of filo pastry on a surface and brush with melted
butter. Repeat the process for all filo sheets. Put the apple mix
on the filo pastry. Roll up the filo to enclose the apple. Brush
with melted butter. Cook in a preheated oven at 190C/374F for
45 minutes.

Christmas Bread

Vanocka

Ingredients

35g/1.2 oz of raisins
35g/1.2 oz of sliced almonds
400g/14 oz of flour
80g/2.8 oz of semolina
35g/1.2 oz of sugar
1 egg
1 teaspoon of vanilla extract
half a tablespoon of lemon zest
160ml/5.4 fl oz of milk
80g/2.8 oz of butter
2 and a quarter teaspoons of yeast
beaten egg

Mix the sugar and flour with a little salt in a bowl. Add half the milk and the yeast. Mix to make a dough. Cover the bowl and leave for 25 minutes.

Melt the butter.

Add the rest of the milk. Add the eggs, raisins, melted butter, lemon zest and vanilla. Knead the dough for 10 minutes. Put the dough in a bowl, cover then leave for 1 hour.

Divide the dough into six pieces. Roll each piece into a long string like shape. Braid the dough springs together. Put on a baking tray. lined with baking/parchment paper. Cover with a damp towel and leave for 1 hour.

Put some beaten egg on top of the cake. Put the almonds on top. Cook in a preheated oven at 180C/356F for 50 minutes.

Rum Balls

Ingredients

120g/4.2 oz of walnuts
120g/4.2 oz of cookies
95g/1 cup of grated coconut
227g/1 cup of butter
300ml/1 and a quarter cups of condensed milk
80ml /2.7 fl oz of rum

Grind the nuts and cookies. Place in a bowl and add the butter and milk. Add the rum and mix to make a dough. Put the dough in the refrigerator for 10 hours.

Roll them into balls and coat in coconut.

Plum Dumplings

Sveskove Knedleky

Ingredients

15 destoned plums
cottage cheese
2 eggs
cinnamon mixed with sugar
2 and a half tablespoons
120ml/half a cup of water
melted butter
salt
half a teaspoon of baking powder

Mix the flour, baking powder, a pinch of salt and water together to make a dough. Wrap the dough around the plums. Put in a pan of boiling water and boil for 15 minutes.

Serve with cottage cheese, melted butter and the sugar mixed with cinnamon.

Czech Christmas Trivia

Like many European nations Christmas markets are very popular in the Czech Republic. They have craft items such as scented candles, wooden toys and jewellery. There are hats, gloves, puppets and dolls. There is a lots of food and drink to sample at the markets such as gingerbread, sweet dumplings, flatbread topped with cheese, barbecued sausages, ham roasted on a pit, Czech beers mulled wine and hot chocolate. The wintry atmosphere and old architecture of many Czech cities and towns make these markets a good Christmas experience.

On the 5th December, which is St Nicholas Eve, St Nicholas visits children with an angel and devil and asks them if they have been good during the year. The good children get fruit or chocolate, the naughty ones get a lump of coal from the devil.

Czechs feel it unlucky to do any laundry on December 24.

On the 25 and 26 of December Czech families meet up. A typical lunch on these days is a roast bird with cabbage and dumplings.

On the On 4 December, St Barbara's Day, a cherry tree branch is picked and put in water. If it blooms by Christmas Eve the pickers wishes will come true the following year.

Vanilla Crescents

Ingredients

117g/2 cups of chopped almonds
283g/10 oz of butter
6 tablespoons of sugar
170g/2 and a quarter cups of flour
2 tablespoons of vanilla extract
1 tablespoon of water
half a teaspoon of salt
confectioners'/icing sugar

Mix the butter, vanilla, water and sugar to make a paste.

Mix the flour and salt and add to the butter mix. Add the nuts.
Make into crescent shapes. Place on parchment paper on a
baking sheet. Cook in a preheated oven at 325F/162C for 20
minutes. Coat in confectioners' sugar.

Gingerbread

Ingredients

2 tablespoons of honey
300g/1 and a half cups of sugar
2 teaspoons of cinnamon
2 teaspoons of dried ginger
1 teaspoon of allspice
1 teaspoon of nutmeg powder
half a teaspoon of baking soda
half a teaspoon of clove powder
200g/1 and a half cups of flour
1 tablespoon of rum
1 teaspoon of lemon zest

Mix the ingredients to form a dough. wrap in clingfilm/plastic wrap and leave for 1 hour.

Roll out the dough. Cut into cookie shapes - for example Christmas cookie shapes can be used. Roll out any excess dough and make more cookie shapes from it. Put on a baking sheet lined with parchment paper and cook in a preheated oven at 325F for 20 minutes.

The gingerbread can be iced.

Bears Paws

Ingredients

85g/3 oz of ground walnuts
half a teaspoon of ground cinnamon
200g/7 oz of butter
3 tablespoons of cocoa powder
290g/10 oz of flour
225g/8 oz of sugar
butter
icing sugar
vanilla extract

Mix the sugar, flour, nuts, cocoa and cinnamon. Add the butter to make a dough. Put the dough in small tin moulds greased with butter- for example shell moulds.

Bake in a preheated oven at 176C/350F for 15 minutes.

Mix some icing sugar with some vanilla extract, and dip the cakes in the mix.

Fruit Cake

Bublanina

Ingredients

700g/1 and a half lb of cherries - with stones taken out
3 egg yolks
3 egg whites
300g/10 oz of flour
230g/8 oz of sugar
230ml/1 cup of milk
pinch of baking powder
2 drops of vanilla extract
butter

Whisk the egg whites and a tablespoon of the sugar together to make a stiff mix.

Mix the egg yolk, vanilla extract and the rest of the sugar and make a stiff batter.

Mix the baking powder and flour and add to the egg yolk mix. Add the egg white mix and fold in.

Butter a baking dish. Add the batter. Put the cherries in the dish. Bake in a preheated oven at 171C/340F for 35 minutes.

Honey Cake

Ingredients

80g/13 oz of walnuts
400ml/1 and a half cups of condensed milk
360g/13 oz of flour
3 eggs
310g/10 oz of sugar
1 tablespoon of baking powder
340g/11 oz of butter
90g/3.1 oz of honey
5 tablespoons of cream

Put the 140g/5 oz of butter, eggs, sugar, cream and honey in a glass bowl. Place over a pan of warm water and mix for 5 minutes.

Mix the flour and baking powder, then add to the other mix to make a dough. Leave for 15 minutes.

Take some parchment/greaseproof paper. Cut into eight 22 cm/9 inch shapes. Roll out bits of the dough and place on the bits of parchment paper. Place on a baking tray and place in a preheated oven at 176C/350F and cook for 8 minutes. Leave to cool.

Put the condensed milk in a pan and cook on a medium heat for 2 hours to make a caramel type sauce. Add the rest of the butter and the walnuts and mix.

Spread the caramel on the pieces of cake and layer.

Potato and Poppy Seed Cones

Ingredients

530g/1.1 lb of boiled and grated potatoes
ground poppy seeds
1 egg
55g/2 oz of semolina
confectioners'/icing sugar
210g/7.5 oz of flour
melted butter

Put the potato, flour, egg, semolina and a pinch of salt in a bowl. Mix to make a dough. Knead for 5 minutes.

Roll out the dough on a floured surface. Make into finger sized pieces. Put in a pan of boiling salted water and cook until they float to the surface.

Drain. Then sprinkle with sugar, melted butter and poppy seeds.

Bombardino

Ingredients

500ml/2 cups of eggnog
210ml/7 fl oz of hot milk
260ml/1 cup of whipping cream
260ml/1 cup of rum
cocoa powder

Put the eggnog and rum in a pan and cook on a low heat for 7 minutes. Add the hot milk and stir. Pour into glasses. Add whipped cream and dust with cocoa.

Eggnog

Ingredients

7 egg yolks
320g/11 oz of sugar
2 packages vanilla sugar or 3 teaspoons of vanilla extract
400g/14 oz of condensed milk
300ml/1 and a quarter cups of milk
500ml/2 cups of rum

Mix the egg yolks and sugar together. Add other ingredients and mix.

Punch

Ingredients

180ml/3 quarters of a cup of brandy
300ml/1 and a quarter cups of red wine
300ml/1 and a quarter cups of water
260g/9 oz of sugar
2 sliced lemons

Mix the brandy, wine, sugar and water in a bowl. Add the lemon.